LIFE IN CHRIST

Morals, Communion and the Church

An Agreed Statement by the
Second Anglican — Roman Catholic
International Commission
A R C I C II

Published for the Anglican Consultative Council and the
Pontifical Council for Promoting Christian Unity

Published 1994 for
The Anglican Consultative Council
157 Waterloo Road, London SE1 8UT

and

The Pontifical Council for Promoting Christian Unity, Vatican City

by Church House Publishing, Church House, Great Smith Street, London SW1P 3NZ

and

Catholic Truth Society 192 Vauxhall Bridge Road, London SW1V 1PD

ISBN 0 7151 4839 7 (CHP)
ISBN 0 85183 911 8 (CTS)

Printed in England by Streetsprinters, Baldock, Herts SG7 6NW

CONTENTS

THE STATUS OF THE DOCUMENT

The Document published here is the work of the Second Anglican-Roman Catholic International Commission (ARCIC II). It is a joint statement of the Commission. The authorities who appointed the Commission have allowed the statement to be published so that it may be widely discussed. It is not an authoritative declaration by the Roman Catholic Church or by the Anglican Communion, who will evaluate the document in order to take a position on it in due time.

Citations from Scripture are mostly from the Revised Standard Version. However, use has also been made of the Jerusalem Bible and the Revised English Bible.

PREFACE

by the Co-Chairmen

As we reach the end of ten years in the life of ARCIC II, it may be opportune to recall the words of Pope John Paul II and Archbishop Robert Runcie in their Common Declaration at Canterbury in May 1982.

> The new International Commission is to continue the work already begun; to examine, especially in the light of our respective judgements on the Final Report, the outstanding doctrinal differences which still separate us; with a view to their eventual resolution; to study all that hinders the mutual recognition of the ministries of our Communions, and to recommend what practical steps will be necessary when, on the basis of our unity in faith, we are able to proceed to the restoration of full communion. We are well aware that this new commission's task will not be easy but we are encouraged by our reliance on the grace of God and by all that we have seen of the power of that grace in the ecumenical movement of our time.

We repeat these words in order to assure both our Communions that the work of the Commission, however long or difficult it may be, must continue and is continuing.

Among the many international dialogues, bilateral and multilateral, between divided Christians, the Anglican - Roman Catholic International Commission is the first to have directly attempted the subject of morals. We have prepared this statement in response to requests from authorities of both our Communions. These requests have given voice to a wide-spread belief that Anglicans and Roman Catholics are as much, if not more, divided on questions of morals as on questions of doctrine. This belief in turn reflects the profound and true conviction that authentic Christian unity is as much a matter of life as of faith. Those who share one faith in Christ will share one life in Christ. Hence the title of this statement: *Life in Christ: Morals, Communion and the Church.*

The theme of this statement was already adumbrated in our previous work on *Church as Communion.* In describing 'the constitutive elements essential for the visible communion of the Church', we wrote: 'Also constitutive of life in communion is acceptance of the same basic moral values, the sharing of the same vision of humanity created in the image of God and re-created in Christ, and the common confession of the one hope in the final consummation of the Kingdom of God' (44, 45).

v

As Christians we seek a common life not for our own sakes only, but for the glory of God and the good of humankind. In the face of the world around us, the name of God is profaned whenever those who call themselves Christians show themselves divided in their witness to the objective moral demands which arise from our life in Christ. Our search for communion and unity in morals as in faith is therefore a form of the Lord's own prayer to his Father;

> Hallowed be thy name,
> thy Kingdom come,
> thy will be done,
> on earth as it is in heaven.

+ CORMAC MURPHY-O'CONNOR
+ MARK SANTER

Venice, 5 September 1993

A   INTRODUCTION

1   There is a popular and widespread belief that the Anglican and Roman Catholic Communions are divided most sharply by their moral teaching. Careful consideration has persuaded the Commission that, despite existing disagreement in certain areas of practical and pastoral judgement, Anglicans and Roman Catholics derive from the Scriptures and Tradition the same controlling vision of the nature and destiny of humanity and share the same fundamental moral values. This substantial area of common conviction calls for shared witness, since both Communions proclaim the same Gospel and acknowledge the same injunction to mission and service. A disproportionate emphasis on particular disagreements blurs this important truth and can provoke a sense of alienation. There is already a notable convergence between the two Communions in the witness they give, for example, on war and peace, euthanasia, freedom and justice, but exaggeration of outstanding differences makes this shared witness – a witness which could give direction to a world in danger of losing its way –more difficult to sustain and at the same time hinders its further development. Such a shared witness is, in today's society, urgent. It is also, we believe, possible. The widespread assumption, therefore, that differences of teaching on certain particular moral issues signify an irreconcilable divergence of under-standing, and therefore present an insurmountable obstacle to shared witness, needs to be countered. Even on those particular issues where disagreement exists, Anglicans and Roman Catholics, we shall argue, share a common perspective and acknowledge the same underlying values. This being so, we question whether the limited disagreement, serious as it is, is itself sufficient to justify a continuing breach of communion.

2   In presenting this statement on morals, we are responding, not simply to popular concern, but also to requests from the authorities of both Communions. In the past, ecumenical dialogue has concentrated on matters of doctrine. These are of primary importance and work here still remains to be done. However, the Gospel we proclaim cannot be divorced from the life we live. Questions of doctrine and of morals are closely inter-connected, and differences in the one area may reflect differences in the other. Common to both is the matter of authority and the manner of its exercise. Although we shall not here be addressing the issue of authority directly, nevertheless we hope that an understanding of the relationship between freedom and authority in the moral life may contribute to our understanding of their relationship in the life of the Church.

1

3   In what follows we shall attempt to display the basis and shape of Christian moral teaching and to show that both our Communions apprehend it in the same light. We begin by reaffirming our common faith that the life to which God, through Jesus Christ, calls women and men is nothing less than participation in the divine life, and we spell out some of the characteristics and implications of our shared vision of life in Christ. We go on to remind ourselves of our common heritage and of the living tradition through which both Communions have sought to develop a faithful and appropriate response to the good news of the Gospel. Next we review the ways in which this tradition has diverged since the break in communion, at the same time drawing attention to signs of a new convergence, not least in our emphasis on the common good. We fasten upon the two particular issues of marriage after divorce and contraception – issues upon which the two Communions have expressed their disagreement in official documents and pastoral practice – in order to determine as precisely as we can the nature and extent of our moral disagreement and to relate it to our continuing agreement on fundamental values. In our last section we return to the theme of communion and, in the light of what has gone before, show how communion determines both the structure of the moral order and the method of the Church's discernment and response. Finally, we reaffirm our belief that differences and disagreements are exacerbated by a continuing breach of communion, and that integrity of moral response itself requires a movement towards full communion. We conclude by suggesting steps by which we may move forward together along this path to the greater glory of God and the well-being of God's world.

B   SHARED VISION

4   The Christian life is a response in the Holy Spirit to God's self-giving in Jesus Christ. To this gift of himself in incarnation, and to this participation in the divine life, the Scriptures bear witness (cf 1 John 1:1-3; 2 Peter 1:3-4). Made in the image of God (cf Gen. 1:27), and part of God's good creation (cf Gen. 1:31), women and men are called to grow into the likeness of God, in communion with Christ and with one another. What has been entrusted to us through the incarnation and the Christian tradition is a vision of God. This vision of God in the face of Jesus Christ (cf 2 Cor. 4:6; compare Gen. 1:3) is at the same time a vision of humanity renewed and fulfilled. Life in Christ is the gift and promise of new creation (cf 2 Cor. 5:17), the ground of community, and the pattern of social relations. It is the shared inheritance of the Church and the hope of every believer.

5   God creates human beings with the dignity of persons in community, calls them to a life of responsibility and freedom, and endows them with the hope of happiness. As children of God, our true freedom is to be found in God's service, and our true happiness in faithful and loving response to God's love and grace. We are created to glorify and enjoy God, and our hearts continue to be restless until they find in God their rest and fulfilment.

6   The true goal of the moral life is the flourishing and fulfilment of that *humanity* for which all men and women have been created. The fundamental moral question, therefore, is not 'What ought we to do?', but 'What kind of persons are we called to become?' For children of God, moral obedience is nourished by the hope of becoming like God (cf 1 John 3:1-3).

7   True personhood has its origins and roots in the life and love of God. The mystery of the divine life cannot be captured by human thought and language, but in speaking of God as Trinity in Unity, Father, Son and Holy Spirit, we are affirming that the Being of God is a unity of self-communicating and interdependent relationships. Human persons, therefore, made in this image, and called to participate in the life of God, may not exercise a freedom that claims to be independent, wilful and self-seeking. Such a use of freedom is a distortion of their God-given humanity. It is sin. The freedom that is properly theirs is a freedom of responsiveness and interdependence. They are created for communion, and communion involves responsibility, in relation to society and nature as well as to God.

8   Ignorance and sin have led to the misuse and corruption of human freedom and to delusive ideas of human fulfilment. But God has been faithful to his eternal purposes of love and, through the redemption of the world by Jesus Christ, offers to human beings participation in a new creation, recalling them to their true freedom and fulfilment. As God remains faithful and free, so those who are in Christ are called to be faithful and free, and to share in God's creative and redemptive work for the whole of creation.

9   The new life in Christ is for the glorification of God. Living in communion with Christ, the Church is called to make Christ's words its own: 'I have glorified you on earth' (cf John 17:4). The new life has also been entrusted to the Church for the good of the whole world (cf. *Church as Communion*, 18). This life is for everyone and embraces everyone. In seeking the common good, therefore, the Church listens and speaks not only to the faithful, but also to women and men of goodwill everywhere. Despite the ambiguities and evils in the world, and despite the sin that has distorted human life, the Church affirms the original goodness of creation and discerns signs and contours of an order that continues to reflect the wisdom and goodness of the Creator. Nor has sin deprived human beings of all perception of this order. It is generally recognised, for example, that torture is intrinsically wrong, and that the integration of sexual instincts and affections into a lifelong relationship of married love and loyalty constitutes a uniquely significant form of human flour-ishing and fulfilment. Reflection on experience of what makes human beings, singly and together, truly human gives rise to a natural morality, sometimes interpreted in terms of natural justice or natural law, to which a general appeal for guidance can be made. In Jesus Christ this natural morality is not denied. Rather, it is renewed, transfigured and perfected, since Christ is the true and perfect image of God.

10   Christian morality is one aspect of the life in Christ which shapes the tradition of the Church, a tradition which is also shaped by the community which carries it. Christian morality is the fruit of faith in God's Word, the grace of the sacraments, and the appropriation, in a life of forgiveness, of the gifts of the Spirit for work in God's service. It manifests itself in the practical teaching and pastoral care of the Church and is the outward expression of that continual turning to God whereby forgiven sinners grow up together into Christ and into the mature humanity of which Christ is the measure and fullness (cf Eph. 4:13). At its deepest level, the response of the Church to the offer of new life in

Christ possesses an unchanging identity from age to age and place to place. In its particular teachings, however, it takes account of changing circumstances and needs, and in situations of unusual ambiguity and perplexity it seeks to combine new insight and discernment with an underlying continuity and consistency.

11 Approached in this light the fundamental questions with which a Christian morality engages are such as these:

What are persons called to be, as individuals and as members one of another in the human family?

What constitutes human dignity, and what are the social as well as the individual dimensions of human dignity and responsibility?

How does divine forgiveness and grace engage with human finitude, fragility and sin in the realisation of human happiness?

How are the conditions and structures of human life related to the goal of human fulfilment?

What are the implications of the creatureliness which human beings share with the rest of the natural world?

At this fundamental level of inquiry and concern, we believe, our two Communions share a common vision and understanding. To affirm our agreement here will prove a significant step forward towards the recovery of full communion. It will put in proper perspective any disagreement that may continue to exist in official teaching and pastoral practice on particular issues, such as divorce and contraception. The crisis of the modern world is more than a crisis of sexual ethics. At stake is our humanity itself.

C   COMMON HERITAGE

1   A Shared Tradition

12   Anglicans and Roman Catholics are conscious that their respective traditions, rooted in a shared vision, stem from a common heritage, which in spite of stress and strain, within and without, shaped the Church's life for some fifteen hundred years. Drawing upon the faith of Israel, this common heritage springs from the conversion of the disciples to faith in Jesus Christ and their mission to share that faith with others. Fullness of life in Christ in the kingdom of God is its goal. It is also the norm by which the tradition in all its varied manifestations is to be judged. Any manifestation that no longer has the power to nurture and sustain the new life in Christ is thereby shown to be corrupt. Anglicans and Roman Catholics firmly believe that their respective traditions continue to nourish and support them in their daily discipleship, but they are aware of the impairment to their common heritage caused by the breach in their communion, and they look forward to the time when both traditions will again flow together for their mutual enrichment and for their common witness and service to the world.

13   The shared tradition was richly woven from many strands. These include faith in God, Father, Son and Holy Spirit, publicly professed in baptism; a common life, founded on love, centred in eucharistic prayer and worship, expressed in service; the teaching and nourishment of the Scriptures; an ordered leadership, entrusted with guarding and guiding the tradition through the conflicts of history; a sense of discipleship, manifested in the lives of the saints and acknowledged by devotion and piety; the proscription of deeds that undermine the values of the Gospel and threaten to destroy the new life in Christ; ways of reconciliation, by which sinners may be brought back into communion with God and with one another. At the same time the tradition drew upon the inherited wisdom and culture of the world in which it was embedded.

14   This common tradition carried with it a 'missionary imperative' – a call to preach the Gospel, to live the life of the Gospel in the world, and to work out a faithful and fruitful response to the Gospel in encounter with different cultures. Both Anglicans and Roman Catholics have understood the missionary task in this way, and both have been eager to fulfil the claims of their earthly citizenship (cf Rom. 13:4-5), while remembering that they are citizens of heaven (cf Phil. 3:20). They have attempted

to carry out Christ's missionary injunction accordingly, though sometimes they have interpreted their involvement in the cultural life of the world in very different ways. In their engagement with culture they have been led to give careful thought to the practical expression of the new life in Christ and to provide specific teaching on some of its moral and social aspects.

15   This openness to the world, which has characterised both our traditions, has shaped the pattern of life which these traditions have sustained. It is not the life of an inwardly pious and self-regarding group, withdrawn from the world and its conflicts. It is, rather, a life to be lived out amidst the ambiguities of the world. Yet it is also a pilgrim life which, while seeking the welfare of the world, has a destiny which transcends the present age. Admittedly, this involvement with the world has from time to time led the Church into compromise and alliance with corrupt principalities and powers. At other times, however, co-operation with secular authorities has borne good fruit, and the conviction that the Church is called to live in the world and to work for the salvation of the world has remained strong. Thus, while both our Communions retain painful memories of occasions of betrayal and sin, both put their trust, not in human strength, but in the saving power of God.

16   Both our traditions draw their vision from the Scriptures. To the Scriptures, therefore, we now turn, to discover the origins of our common heritage in the Gospel of Jesus Christ and the faithful response of the Christian community.

2   The Pattern of Our Life in Christ

17   The good news of the Gospel is the coming of the kingdom of God (cf Mark 1:15), the redemption of the world by our Lord Jesus Christ (cf Gal. 4:4-5), the forgiveness of sins and new life in the Spirit (cf Acts 2:38), and the hope of glory (cf Col. 1:27).

18   The redemption won by Jesus Christ carries with it the promise of a new life of freedom from the domination of sin (cf Rom. 6:18). Through his dying on the cross Christ has overcome the powers of darkness and death, and through his rising again from the dead he has opened the gates of eternal life (cf Heb. 10:19-22). No longer are men and women alienated from God and from one another, enslaved by sin, abandoned to despair and destined to destruction (cf Eph. 2:1-12). The entail of sin has been broken and humanity set free – free to enter upon the liberty and splendour of the children of God (cf Rom. 6:23; 8:21).

19   The liberty promised to the children of God is nothing less than participation, with Christ and through the Holy Spirit, in the life of God. The gift of the Spirit is the pledge and first instalment of the coming kingdom (cf 2 Cor. 1:21-22). Patterned according to Christ, the Wisdom of God, and empowered by the Holy Spirit of God, the Church is called not only to proclaim God's kingdom, but also to be the sign and first-fruits of its coming. The unity, holiness, catholicity and apostolicity of the Church derive their meaning and reality from the meaning and reality of God's kingdom. They reflect the fullness of the life of God. They are signs of the universal love of God, Father, Son and Holy Spirit, the love poured out upon the whole creation. Hence the life of the Church, the body of Christ, the community of the Holy Spirit, is rooted and grounded in the eternal life and love of God.

20   It is this patterning power of the kingdom that gives the Church its distinctive character (cf Rom. 14:17). The new humanity, which the Gospel makes possible, is present in the community of those who, already belonging to the new world inaugurated by the resurrection, live according to the law of the Spirit written in their hearts (cf Jer. 31:33). However, the Church has always to become more fully what its title deeds proclaim it to be. It exists in the 'between-time', between the coming of Christ in history and his coming again as the Christ of glory. In so far as it remains in the world, it too has to learn obedience to its living Lord, and to work out in its own life in community the matter and manner of its discipleship.

21   The earliest disciples devoted themselves to the 'apostles' teaching and fellowship, the breaking of bread and the prayers' (Acts 2:42). In the portrayal of this communion the disciples were said to have had 'all things in common', selling their possessions and sharing their goods 'as any had need' (Acts 2:44-45). This striking example of community care and concern has, down the ages, prompted a critique of every form of society based on the unbridled pursuit of wealth and power. It has challenged Christians to use their gifts and resources to equip God's people for the work of service (cf Eph. 4:12). Its deep significance is disclosed in the claim that the whole company of believers was 'of one heart and soul . . . and everything they owned was held in common' (Acts 4:32).

22   This communion in heart and soul is inspired by the Holy Spirit and manifested in a life patterned according to the mind of Christ. As Paul puts it, 'if there is any encouragement in Christ, any incentive of love, any participation in the Spirit, any affection and sympathy, complete my joy by being of the same mind, having the same love, being in full accord and

of one mind . . . that same mind which was in Christ Jesus' (Phil. 2:1-2, 5). The distinctive mark of the mind of Christ, Paul goes on to explain, is humble obedience and self-emptying love (cf Phil. 2:7-8).

3   The Mind of Christ

23   The mind of Christ remains in the Church through the presence of the Paraclete/Spirit (cf John 14:26). It is mediated through the remembered teaching of Jesus and the prayerful discernment of the body of Christ and its members, and gives shape and direction to the practical life of the Christian community. This teaching is expressed in Jesus' summary of the Law in the twofold commandment of love (cf Matt. 22:37-40), and spelled out in the Sermon on the Mount, especially the Beatitudes and the reinterpretation of the Commandments (cf Matt. 5:3-12, 21-48). It has a dual focus in the radical command 'Love your enemies' (cf Matt. 5:43) and the new commandment 'Love one another as I have loved you' (cf John 13:34). The mind of Christ, so disclosed, determines the character of renewed humanity, forms the pattern of Christian obedience, and establishes the universe of shared moral values. In this important sense there is a givenness within the Christian response, which the changes of history and culture cannot impair.

24   The mind of Christ, who is the Way as well as the Truth and the Life (cf John 14:6; Matt. 7:14), also shapes the process by which Christians approach the challenge of new and complex moral and pastoral problems. Because they worship the same God and follow the same Lord, with the guidance of the Holy Spirit they approach these problems with similar resources and concerns. The method of arriving at practical decisions may vary, but underlying any differences of method there is a shared understanding of the need to use practical reason in interpreting the witness of the Scriptures, tradition and experience.

25   The mind of Christ also exposes the continuing threat of sin - sins of ignorance and neglect as well as deliberate sins. A knowing and willing disregard of the pattern of life which Christ sets before us is deliberate sin. But people can also drift into sin without any clear perception of what they are doing. Distorted structures of common life prompt a sinful response. Habits of sin then dull the conscience, until sinners come to prefer darkness to light. So solidarity in sin threatens to disrupt the fellowship of the Holy Spirit.

26   In Christ freedom and order are mutually supportive. The obedience
of Christian discipleship is neither the mechanical application of regula-
tion and rule, nor the wilful decision of arbitrary choice. In the freedom
of a faithful and obedient response the disciples of Christ seek to discern
Christ's mind rather than express their own. In exercising its authority
to remit and retain sins (cf John 20:23), the Church has a twofold task: of
guarding against the power of sin to destroy the life of the community,
and of fostering the freedom of its members to discern what is 'good and
acceptable and perfect' (Rom. 12:2).

4 Growing up into Christ

27   The salvation which God has secured for us once and for all, through
the death and resurrection of Jesus Christ, he has now to secure in us and
with us through the power of the Holy Spirit. We have to become what,
in Christ, we already are. We have to 'grow up in every way into him who
is the head, into Christ' (Eph. 4:15). We have to 'work out (our) own
salvation with fear and trembling; for God is at work in (us), both to will
and to work for his good pleasure' (Phil. 2:12-13).

28   The lived response of the Church to the grace of God develops its
own shape and character. The pattern of this response is fashioned
according to the mind of Christ; the raw material is the stuff of our
everyday world. In Johannine language, believers are still 'in' the world,
but are not 'of' the world (cf John 17:13-14). In Pauline language, they
continue to live 'in the body' (2 Cor. 5:6), but no longer 'in the flesh'
(Rom. 8:9). Christians are to continue in their secular roles and relationships according to the accepted social codes of behaviour, but are to do
so as 'in the Lord' (cf Eph. 5:21–6:11; Col. 3:18–4:1). Their new intention
and motivation, while affirming the need for these social structures,
contain the seeds of radical critique and reappraisal.

29   The fidelity of the Church to the mind of Christ involves a
continuing process of listening, learning, reflecting and teaching. In this
process every member of the community has a part to play. Each person
learns to reflect and act according to conscience. Conscience is informed
by, and informs, the tradition and teaching of the community. Learning
and teaching are a shared discipline, in which the faithful seek to discover
together what obedience to the gospel of grace and the law of love entails
amidst the moral perplexities of the world. It is this task of discovering
the moral implications of the Gospel which calls for continuing discern-

ment, constant repentance and 'renewal of the mind' (Rom. 12:2), so that through discernment and response men and women may become what in Christ they already are.

30 As part of its missionary imperative and pastoral care, the Church has not only to hand on from generation to generation its understanding of life in Christ, but also from time to time to determine how best to reconcile and support those members of the community who have, for whatever reason, failed to live up to its moral demands. Its aim is twofold: on the one hand, both to minimise the harm done by their falling away and to maintain the integrity of the community; and on the other, to restore the sinner to the life of grace in the fellowship of the Church.

5 Discerning the Mind of Christ

31 Christian morality is an authentic expression of the new life lived in the power of the Holy Spirit and fashioned according to the mind of Christ. In the tradition common to both our Communions, discerning the mind of Christ is a patient and continuing process of prayer and reflection. At its heart is the turning of the sinner to God, sacramentally enacted in baptism and renewed through participation in the sacramental life of the Church, meditation on the scriptures, and a life of daily discipleship. The process unfolds through the formation of a character, individual and communal, that reflects the likeness of Christ and embodies the virtues of a true humanity (cf Gal. 5:19-24). At the same time shared values are formulated in terms of principles and rules defining duties and protecting rights. All this finds expression in the common life of the Church as well as in its practical teaching and pastoral care.

32 The teaching developed in this way is an essential element in the process by which individuals and communities exercise their discernment on particular moral issues. Holding in mind the teaching they have received, drawing upon their own experience, and exploring the particularities of the issue that confronts them, they have then to decide what action to take in these circumstances and on this occasion. Such a decision is not only a matter of deduction. Nor can it be taken in isolation. It also calls for detailed and accurate assessment of the facts of the case, careful and consistent reflection and, above all, sensitivity of insight inspired by the Holy Spirit.

6 Continuity and Change

33   Guided by the Holy Spirit, believer and believing community seek to discern the mind of Christ amidst the changing circumstances of their own histories. Fidelity to the Gospel, obedience to the mind of Christ, openness to the Holy Spirit – these remain the source and strength of continuity. Where communities have separated, traditions diverge; and it is only to be expected that a difference of emphasis in moral judgement will also occur. Where there has been an actual break in communion, this difference cannot but be the more pronounced, giving rise to the impression, often mistaken, that there is some fundamental disagreement of understanding and approach.

34   Moral discernment is a demanding task both for the community and for the individual Christian. The more complex the particular issue, the greater the room for disagreement. Christians of different communions are more likely to agree on the character of the Christian life and the fundamental Christian virtues and values. They are more likely to disagree on the consequent rules of practice, particular moral judgements and pastoral counsel.

35   In this chapter we have been concerned to reaffirm the heritage which Anglicans and Roman Catholics share together. We believe that the elements of this heritage provide the basis for a common witness to the world. But since the Reformation the traditions of our two Communions have diverged, and there are now differences between them which we must acknowledge and face with honesty and patience. Left unacknowledged, they remain a threat to any common task we might undertake. Faced together with honesty and integrity, they will, we believe, be seen at a deeper level to reflect different aspects of a living whole.

D PATHS DIVERGE

36   For some fifteen centuries the Church in the West struggled to maintain a single, living tradition of communion in worship, faith and practice. In the sixteenth century, however, this web of shared experience was violently broken. Movements for reform could no longer be contained within the one Communion. The Roman Catholic Church and the Churches of the Reformation went their different ways and fruits of shared communion were lost. It is in this context of broken communion and diverging histories that the existing differences between Anglicans and Roman Catholics on matters of morality must be located if they are to be rightly understood.

37   These differences, we believe, do not derive from disagreement on the sources of moral authority or on fundamental moral values. Rather, they have arisen from the different emphases which our two Communions have given to different elements of the moral life. In particular, differences have occurred in the ways in which each, in isolation from the other, has developed its structures of authority and has come to exercise that authority in the formation of moral judgement. These factors, we believe, have contributed significantly to the differences that have arisen in a limited number of important moral issues. We cannot, of course, hope to do justice to the complex histories that have shaped our two Communions and given to each its distinctive ethos. However, we wish to draw attention to two strands in our histories which, for present purposes, are of special significance: first, structures of government and the voice of the laity; and secondly, processes of moral formation and individual judgement.

1 Structures of Government and the Voice of the Laity

38   At the Reformation the Church of England abjured papal supremacy, acknowledged the Sovereign as its Supreme Governor (cf Article 37), and adopted English as the language of its liturgy (cf Article 24). Thus the life of the Church, the culture of the nation and the law of the land were inextricably combined. In particular, the lay voice was given, through Parliament, a substantial measure of authority in the affairs of the Church. With the growth of the Anglican Communion as a world-wide body, patterns of synodical government developed in which laity, clergy and bishops shared the authority of government, the bishops retaining a special voice and responsibility in safeguarding matters of doctrine and worship.

13

39   As the Anglican Communion has spread, provinces independent of the Church of England have come into being, each with its own history and culture. English culture has become less and less of a common bond as other cultures have exercised an increasing influence. Each province is responsible for the ordering of its own life and has independent legislative and juridical authority; yet each continues in communion with the Church of England and with one another. Every ten years since 1867 the bishops of the Anglican Communion have met together at Lambeth at the invitation of the Archbishop of Canterbury, to whom they continue to ascribe a primacy of honour. The resolutions of their conferences have a high degree of authority, but they do not become the official teaching of the individual provinces until these have formally ratified them. In recent times regular meetings of the Primates of the Anglican Communion, as well as of the Anglican Consultative Council, in which laity, clergy and bishops are all represented, have contributed to this network of dispersed authority. Whether existing instruments of unity in the Anglican Communion will prove adequate to the task of preserving full communion between the provinces, as they develop their moral teaching in a rapidly changing and deeply perplexing world, remains to be seen.

40   The Reformation and its aftermath also had repercussions in the government of the Roman Catholic Church. Some of the European rulers who maintained allegiance to Rome found this relationship strained and frustrating, especially since, in certain areas, the papacy also exercised temporal power. The Church reacted strongly, however, to any attempt by a secular power to arrogate to itself prerogatives that it believed were rightfully its own. This concern of the Church to uphold its independence from the state, together with its need to reaffirm and strengthen its unity in the face of divisive forces, lent to the papal office a renewed significance, and provided the context for the solemn definition of the first Vatican Council which clarified the universal jurisdiction of the Bishop of Rome and his infallibility.

41   A further development in the Roman Catholic Church since Vatican I has clarified the teaching role of the college of bishops in communion with its head, the bishop of Rome. Bishops are not only the chief teachers in their own dioceses, but they also share responsibility for the teaching of the whole Church. For Roman Catholics, government and teaching continue to be the prerogative of the episcopal office. Their experience has been that these structures of authority have served the Church well in maintaining a fundamental unity of moral teaching.

42   There has also been a significant development in the Roman Catholic Church in the ways by which the laity participate in the discernment and articulation of the Church's faith. Lay persons have taken on new roles in liturgy, catechesis and pastoral work, and have come to be involved with their pastors in a variety of consultative and advisory bodies at parochial, diocesan and national levels. This collaboration has been enhanced by their involvement in theological education.

2 Processes of Moral Formation and Individual Judgement

43   After the breakdown in communion, Anglicans and Roman Catholics continued to develop, in related but distinctive ways, their common tradition of moral theology and its application by a process of casuistry to specific moral problems. This process has its roots in the New Testament and the writings of the Church Fathers. In the late Middle Ages, however, certain widespread philosophical views diverted attention from the controlling moral vision and concentrated on the obligations of the individual will and the legality of particular acts. What was intended to be a painstaking search for the will of God in the complex circumstances of daily life ran the danger of becoming either meticulous moralism or a means of minimising the challenge of the Gospel.

44   Developments in Roman Catholic moral theology after the Council of Trent were not altogether free from this danger. In the seventeenth century papal authority countermanded both rigorism and laxity. It sought to re-establish a vision of the moral life which respected the demands of the Gospel while, at the same time, acknowledging the costliness of discipleship and the frailties of the human condition. During this and subsequent periods, moral theology and spiritual theology were treated as two distinct disciplines, the former tending to restrict itself to the minimal requirements of Christian obedience. In the second half of the present century the Roman Catholic Church, in its desire to set the moral life within a comprehensive vision of life in the Spirit, has witnessed a renewal of moral theology. There has been a return to the Scriptures as the central source of moral insight. Older discussions, based on the natural law, with the Scriptures cited solely for confirmation, have been integrated into a more personalistic account of the moral life, which itself has been grounded in the vocation of all human persons to participate in the life of God. An emphasis on the community of persons has led to significant developments, not only in the Church's teaching on personal relation-

ships, but also in its teaching on the economic and social implications of the common good.

45 The Anglican tradition of moral theology has been varied and heterogeneous. In the seventeenth century Anglican theologians of both catholic and puritan persuasion produced comprehensive works of 'practical divinity'. Drawing on the scholastic tradition, and determined to hold together the moral and spiritual life, they developed this tradition within a context of the Christian vocation to personal holiness. Thus they rejected any approach to the moral life that smacked of moral laxity, and mistrusted any casuistry that, in the details of its analysis of the moral act, threatened to destroy an integral spirit of genuine repentance and renewal. In subsequent centuries the practice of casuistry fell largely into disuse, to be replaced by teaching on 'Christian ethics'. The aim of this discipline was to set forth the ideal character and pattern of the Christian life and so to prepare Christians for making their own decisions how best to realise that ideal in their own circumstances. The present century has seen a renewal among Anglicans of the discipline of moral theology, sustained by a growing recognition of the need for systematic reflection on the difficult moral issues raised by new technologies, the limits of natural resources and the claims of the natural environment. In recent times, in response to widespread appeals for guidance on issues of public and social morality, representatives of Christian bodies and other persons of good will have been brought together to study these issues and to suggest how society might best respond to them for the sake of the common good.

46 Anglicans and Roman Catholics have both used a variety of means to strengthen Christian discipleship in its moral dimension. These have included preaching, regular use of catechisms, and public recitation of the Commandments. In one matter of special significance, however, the Reformation and the consequent Counter-Reformation moved the Church of England and the Roman Catholic Church in different directions. The Reformers' emphasis on the direct access of the sinner to the forgiving and sustaining Word of God led Anglicans to reject the view that private confession before a priest was obligatory, although they continued to maintain that it was a wholesome means of grace, and made provision for it in the Book of Common Prayer for those with an unquiet and sorely troubled conscience. While many Anglicans value highly the practice of private confession to a priest, others believe with equal sincerity that it is for them unhelpful and unnecessary. It is sufficient for themselves, they say, that the Word of God, expressed in the Scriptures and appropriated

in the power of the Holy Spirit, speaks authoritatively to their conscience, offering both assurance of forgiveness and practical guidance. For both those who do, and for those who do not, confess their sins privately, general confession and absolution by the priest remains an integral part of the regular Anglican liturgy, a ministry designed to cover both individual and corporate sin. Furthermore, Anglicans often turn to their pastors and advisers, lay and ordained, for moral and spiritual counsel.

47   The Roman Catholic Church, on the other hand, has continued to emphasise the sacrament of penance and the obligation, for those conscious of serious sin, of confessing their sins privately before a priest. Indeed, the renewal of private confession was a major concern of the Council of Trent. Since Vatican II the development of the ministry of forgiveness and healing has led to new forms of sacramental reconciliation, both individual and communal. For centuries the discipline of the confession of sins before a priest has provided an important means of communicating the Church's moral teaching and nurturing the spiritual lives of penitents.

3 Moral Judgement and the Exercise of Authority

48   Reflection on the divergent histories of our two Communions has shown that their shared concern to respond obediently to God's Word and to foster the common good has nevertheless resulted in differing emphases in the ways in which they have nurtured Christian liberty and exercised Christian authority. Both Communions recognise that liberty and authority are essentially interdependent, and that the exercise of authority is for the protection and nurture of liberty. It cannot be denied, however, that there is a continuing temptation – a temptation which the continued separation of our two Communions serves only to accentuate – to allow the exercise of authority to lapse into authoritarianism and the exercise of liberty to lapse into individualism.

49   All moral authority is grounded in the goodness and will of God. Our two Communions are agreed on this principle and on its implications. Both our Communions, moreover, have developed their own structures and institutions for the teaching ministry of the Church, by which the will of God is discerned and its implications for the common good declared. Our Communions have diverged, however, in their views of the ways in which authority is most fruitfully exercised and the common good best promoted. Anglicans affirm that authority needs to

be dispersed rather than centralised, that the common good is better served by allowing to individual Christians the greatest possible liberty of informed moral judgement, and that therefore official moral teaching should as far as possible be commendatory rather than prescriptive and binding. Roman Catholics, on the other hand, have, for the sake of the common good, emphasised the need for a central authority to preserve unity and to give clear and binding teaching.

4 Differing Emphases, Shared Perspectives

50   In our conversations together we have made two discoveries: first, that many of the preconceptions that we brought with us concerning each other's understanding of moral teaching and discipline were often little more than caricatures; and secondly, that the differences which actually exist between us appear in a new light when we consider them in their origin and context.

51   Some of these differences lend themselves to misperception and caricature. It is not true, for instance, that Anglicans concern themselves solely with liberty, while Roman Catholics concern themselves solely with law. It is not true that the Roman Catholic Church has predetermined answers to every moral question, while the Anglican Church has no answers at all. It is not true that Roman Catholics always agree on moral issues, nor that Anglicans never agree. It is not true that Anglican ethics is pragmatic and unprincipled, while Roman Catholic moral theology is principled but abstract. It is not true that Roman Catholics are always more careful of the institution in their concern for the common good, while Anglicans disregard the common good in their concern for the individual. It is not true that Roman Catholic moral teaching is legalistic, while Anglican moral teaching is utilitarian. Caricature, we may grant, is never totally contrived; but caricature it remains. In fact, there is good reason to hope that, if they can pray, think and act together, Anglicans and Roman Catholics, by emphasising different aspects of the moral life, may come to complement and enrich each other's understanding and practice of it.

52   Nevertheless, differences there are and differences they remain. Both Anglicans and Roman Catholics are accustomed to using the concept of law to give character and form to the claims of morality. However, this concept is open to more than one interpretation and use, so causing real and apparent differences between our two traditions. For example, a

notable feature of established Roman Catholic moral teaching is its emphasis on the absoluteness of some demands of the moral law and the existence of certain prohibitions to which there are no exceptions. In these instances, what is prohibited is intrinsically disordered and therefore objectively wrong. Anglicans, on the other hand, while acknowledging the same ultimate values, are not persuaded that the laws as we apprehend them are necessarily absolute. In certain circumstances, they would argue, it might be right to incorporate contextual and pastoral considerations in the formulation of a moral law, on the grounds that fundamental moral values are better served if the law sometimes takes into account certain contingencies of nature and history and certain disorders of the human condition. In so doing, they do not make the clear-cut distinction, which Roman Catholics make, between canon law, with its incorporation of contingent and prudential considerations, and the moral law, which in its principles is absolute and universal. In both our Communions, however, there are now signs of a shift away from a reliance on the concept of law as the central category for providing moral teaching. Its place is being taken by the concept of 'persons-in-community'. An ethic of response is preferred to an ethic of obedience. In the desire to respond as fully as possible to the new law of Christ, the primacy of persons is emphasised above the impersonalism of a system of law, thus avoiding the distortions of both individualism and utilitarianism. The full significance of this shift of emphasis is not yet clear, and its detailed implications have still to be worked out. It should be emphasised, however, that whatever differences there may be in the way in which they express the moral law, both our traditions respect the consciences of persons in good faith.

53   We hope we have said enough in this chapter to explain how a deeper understanding of our separated histories has enabled us to appreciate better the real character of our divergences, and has persuaded us that it has been our broken communion, more than anything else, that has exacerbated our disagreements. In recent times there has been a large measure of cross-fertilisation between our two traditions. Both our Communions, for example, have shared in the renewal of biblical, historical and liturgical studies, and both have participated in the ecumenical movement. Our separated paths have once again begun to converge. It is in the conviction that we also possess a shared vision of Christian discipleship and a common approach to the moral life, that we take courage now to look directly at our painful disagreement on two particular moral issues.

E   AGREEMENT AND DISAGREEMENT

54   The two moral issues on which the Anglican and Roman Catholic Communions have expressed official disagreement are: the marriage of a divorced person during the life-time of a former partner; and the permissible methods of controlling conception. There are other issues concerning sexuality on which Anglican and Roman Catholic attitudes and opinions appear to conflict, especially abortion and the exercise of homosexual relations. These we shall consider briefly at the end of this section; but because of the official nature of the disagreement on the former two issues, we shall concentrate on them.

1 Human Sexuality

55   Before considering the points of disagreement, we need to emphasise the extent of our agreement. Both our traditions affirm with Scripture that human sexuality is part of God's good creation (cf Gen. 1:27; see further Gen. 24; Ruth 4; the Song of Songs; Eph. 5:21-32; etc.). Sexual differentiation within the one human nature gives bodily expression to the vocation of God's children to inter-personal communion. Human sexuality embraces the whole range of bodily, imaginative, affective and spiritual experience. It enters into a person's deepest character and relationships, individual and social, and constitutes a fundamental mode of human communication. It is ordered towards the gift of self and the creation of life.

56   Sexual experience, isolated from the vision of the full humanity to which God calls us, is ambivalent. It can be as disruptive as it can be unitive, as destructive as it can be creative. Christians have always known this to be so (cf Matt. 5:28). They have therefore recognised the need to integrate sexuality into an ordered pattern of life, which will nurture a person's spiritual relationships both with other persons and with God. Such integration calls for the exercise of the virtue traditionally termed chastity, a virtue rooted in the spiritual significance of bodily existence (cf 1 Thess. 4:1-8; Gal. 5:23; 1 Cor. 6:9, 12-20).

57   Both our traditions offer comparable accounts of chastity, which involves the ordering of the sexual drive either towards marriage or in a life of celibacy. Chastity does not signify the repression of sexual instincts and energies, but their integration into a pattern of relationships in which

a person may find true happiness, fulfilment and salvation. Anglicans and Roman Catholics agree that the new life in Christ calls for a radical break with the sin of sexual self-centredness, which leads inevitably to individual and social disintegration. The New Testament is unequivocal in its witness that the right ordering and use of sexual energy is an essential aspect of life in Christ (cf Mark 10:9; John 8:11; 1 Cor. 7; 1 Peter 3:1-7; Heb. 13:4), and this is reiterated throughout the common Christian tradition, including the time since our two Communions diverged.

58   Human beings, male and female, flourish as persons in community. Personal relationships have a social as well as a private dimension. Sexual relationships are no exception. They are bound up with issues of poverty and justice, the equality and dignity of women and men, and the protection of children. Both our traditions treat of human sexuality in the context of the common good, and regard marriage and family life as institutions divinely appointed for human well-being and happiness. It is in the covenanted relationship between husband and wife that the physical expression of sexuality finds its true fulfilment (cf Gen. 2:18-25), and in the procreation and nurturing of children that the two persons together share in the life-giving generosity of God (cf Gen. 1:27-29).

2 Marriage and Family

59   Neither of our two traditions regards marriage as a human invention. On the contrary, both see it as grounded by God in human nature and as a source of community, social order and stability. Nevertheless, the institution of marriage has found different expression in different cultures and at different times. In our own time, for instance, we are becoming increasingly aware that some forms, far from nurturing the dignity of persons, foster oppression and domination, especially of women. However, despite the distortions that have affected it, both our traditions continue to discern and uphold in marriage a God-given pattern and significance.

60   Marriage gives rise to enduring obligations. Personal integrity and social witness both require a life-long and exclusive commitment, and the 'goods' which marriage embodies include the reciprocal love of husband and wife, and the procreation and raising of children. When these realities are disregarded, a breakdown of family life may ensue, carrying with it a heavy burden of misery and social disintegration. The word 'obligation', however, is inadequate to express the profound personal call inherent in

the Christian understanding of marriage. Both our traditions speak of marriage as a vocation: as a 'vocation to holiness' (Lambeth 1958, Resolution 112 as quoted in Lambeth 1968, Resolution 22), as involving an 'integral vision of ... vocation' (*Familiaris Consortio*, 32). When God calls women and men to the married estate, and supports them in it, God's love for them is creative, redemptive and sanctifying (cf Lambeth, ibid.).

61   The mutual pact, or covenant, made between the spouses (cf *Gaudium et Spes*, 47-52, and *Final Report on the Theology of Marriage and its Application to Mixed Marriages*, 1975, 21) bears the mark of God's own abundant love (cf Hosea 2:19-21). Covenanted human love points beyond itself to the covenantal love and fidelity of God and to God's will that marriage should be a means of universal blessing and grace. Marriage, in the order of creation, is both sign and reality of God's faithful love, and thus it has a naturally sacramental dimension. Since it also points to the saving love of God, embodied in Christ's love for the Church (cf Eph. 5:25), it is open to a still deeper sacramentality within the life and communion of Christ's own Body.

62   So far, we believe, our traditions agree. Further discussion, however, is needed on the ways in which they interpret this sacramentality of marriage. The Roman Catholic tradition, following the common tradition of the West, which was officially promulgated by the Council of Florence in 1439, affirms that Christian marriage is a sacrament in the order of redemption, the natural sign of the human covenant having been raised by Christ to become a sign of the irrevocable covenant between himself and his Church. What was sacramental in the order of creation becomes a sacrament of the Church in the order of redemption. When solemnised between two baptised persons, marriage is an effective sign of redeeming grace. Anglicans, while affirming the special significance of marriage within the Body of Christ, emphasise a sacramentality of marriage that transcends the boundaries of the Church. For many years in England after the Reformation, marriages could be solemnised only in church. When civil marriage became possible, Anglicans recognised such marriages, too, as sacramental and graced by God, since the state of matrimony had itself been 'adorned and beautified' by Christ by his presence at the marriage at Cana of Galilee (cf *BCP 1662, Introduction to the Solemnization of Matrimony*). From these considerations it would appear that, in this context, Anglicans tend to emphasise the breadth of God's grace in creation, while Roman Catholics tend to emphasise the depth of God's grace in Christ. These emphases should be seen as

complementary. Ideally, they belong together. They have, however, given rise to differing understandings of the conditions under which the sacramentality of a marriage is fulfilled.

63   The vision of marriage as a fruitful, life-long covenant, full of the grace of God, is not always sustained in the realities of life. Its very goodness, when corrupted by human frailty, self-centredness and sin, gives rise to pain, despair and tragedy, not only for the couple immediately involved in marital difficulty or breakdown, but also for their children, the wider family and the social order. Faced with such situations, the Church endeavours to minister the grace and discipline of Christ himself. Anglicans and Roman Catholics have both sought to act in obedience to the teaching of Christ. However, in their separation their practice and pastoral discipline came to differ and diverge. In order to elucidate the significance of such differences and divergences we shall now turn to the two issues on which disagreement has been officially voiced, namely, marriage after divorce, and contraception.

3 Marriage After Divorce

64   Before the break in communion in the sixteenth century, the Church in the West had come to derive a doctrine of indissolubility from its interpretation of the teaching of Jesus concerning marriage. The official Church teaching included two affirmations: not only was it the case that the marriage bond *ought not* to be dissolved; but it was also the case that it *could not* be dissolved. At the Reformation, continental Protestant Reformers interpreted the teaching of Jesus (cf Matt. 5:32; 19:9) differently, and argued that divorce was permissible on grounds of adultery or desertion. The Council of Trent, on the other hand, reaffirmed the teaching, first, that the marriage bond could not be dissolved, even by adultery and secondly, that neither partner, not even the innocent one, could contract a second marriage during the life-time of the other.

(a) The Anglican Communion

65   The development of a distinctive marriage discipline within Anglicanism can be understood only in the context of the development of diverse civil jurisdictions. This is true both of the Church of England and of other Anglican provinces. At the time of the Reformation the Church of England passed no formal resolution on marriage and divorce. It never

23

officially accepted the teaching of the continental Reformers but, despite attempts to introduce an alternative discipline, held to the older belief and practice. Revisions of Canon Law in 1597 and 1604 established no change in teaching or discipline, although, in the centuries that followed, theological opinion varied and even practice was not completely uniform. Up to the middle of the nineteenth century divorce, with the consequent freedom to marry again, was available only to the rich and influential few by Act of Parliament. In 1857, when matrimonial matters were transferred from ecclesiastical to civil jurisdiction, divorce on grounds of adultery was legalised. Although clergy were given the right to refuse to solemnise the marriage of a divorced person in the lifetime of a former partner, the Church of England as a whole came to accept *de facto* the new state of affairs: marriages after divorce occurred, but the Church refused to give official approval to their solemnisation.

66   As Anglican Provinces were inaugurated outside England, each had to formulate its own pastoral marriage discipline in the light of local civil law and marriage customs. In an attempt to secure a coherent policy among the provinces, the Lambeth Conference of 1888 reaffirmed the life-long intention of the marriage covenant, but accepted that the clergy should not be instructed to refuse the sacraments to those who were remarried 'under civil sanction'. It left open the question whether or not the innocent party was free to enter a second marriage. Since then, theological opinion has varied. Some Anglicans have continued to hold the traditional view of indissolubility. Others have argued that, once the married relationship has been destroyed beyond repair, the marriage itself is as if dead, the vows have been frustrated and the bond has been broken. The Lambeth Conference of 1978 reaffirmed the 'first-order principle' of life-long union, but it also acknowledged a responsibility for those for whom '*no* course *absolutely* consonant with the first-order principle of marriage as a life-long union may be available' (Resolution 34). Subsequent practice has varied. Different provinces of the Anglican Communion have devised different marriage disciplines. Among some of them permission is granted, on carefully considered pastoral grounds, for a marriage after divorce to be solemnised in church, although even in these cases practice varies concerning the precise form the complete service takes. In other cases, after a civil ceremony, a service of prayer and dedication may be offered instead. The practical decision normally lies with the bishop and the bishop's advisers.

(b) The Roman Catholic Church

67 In the period following the breach of communion, the Roman Catholic Church continued to uphold the doctrine of indissolubility reaffirmed at Trent. At the same time it developed a complex system of jurisprudence and discipline to meet its diverse practical and pastoral needs and to provide a supportive role for those whose faith was threatened by a destructive marital relationship.

68 A distinction is made between marriages that are sacraments – those in which both partners are baptised – and marriages that are not sacraments ('natural' marriages) – those in which one or both partners are unbaptised. In Roman Catholic teaching both forms of marriage are in principle indissoluble. A sacramental marriage which has been duly consummated cannot be dissolved by any human power, civil or ecclesiastical. Where such a marriage, however, has not been consummated, it can be dissolved. On the other hand, it has come to be accepted that a non-sacramental marriage, whether consummated or not, can in certain cases be dissolved.

69 The history of these matters is long and complex. In his first letter to the Corinthians, St Paul deals with the case of a married couple, one of whom is a believer, the other a non-believer. If the non-believer refuses to stay with the believer, then, he says, 'the brother or sister is not bound' (1 Cor. 7:15; cf 12-15). This was later interpreted in Canon Law to mean that the partner who had become a Christian was free to leave an unbelieving spouse who was unwilling to continue married life 'in peace', and to marry again. There are several references to this 'Pauline text' in the writings of the early Church Fathers dealing with the dissolution of marriage. It became part of church legislation in 1199, but was fully clarified only in the Code of Canon Law of 1917. It is still part of Roman Catholic practice (cf *Codex Iuris Canonici* [CIC] Can. 1143).

70 The exercise of the 'Pauline privilege' is not the only occasion when the power to dissolve a marriage is invoked. In the course of the missionary expansion of the Church other situations have prompted similar action. From 1537 Popes used their powers to dissolve the natural marriages of inhabitants of Africa and the Indies who wished to convert to the Catholic faith. In 1917 this practice 'in favour of the faith' (or, as it is sometimes called, the 'Petrine privilege') was extended to other parts of the world and applied to similar situations. The 'privilege of the faith' is still recognised today, and subject to certain conditions, a dissolution of a

non-sacramental marriage may, by way of exception, be granted on these grounds by the Holy See.

71   Other elements in Roman Catholic doctrine and practice have been prompted by particular practical problems. For example, it was the problem of clandestine marriages, valid but not proved to be so, that prompted the Council of Trent to promulgate the decree *Tametsi* (1563). This required that marriages be celebrated before the pastor (or another priest delegated by him or the ordinary) and two or three witnesses. With certain modifications, this 'form' is still binding, and failure to observe it, without due dispensation, renders a marriage null and void (cf CIC Can. 1108). A partner to such a union, therefore, is not considered in Canon Law to be held by a marital bond and is free to contract a valid marriage. In the case of an intended marriage between a Roman Catholic and a person who is not a Roman Catholic, the Church today often grants a dispensation from the 'form', out of respect for the beliefs, conscience and family ties of the person concerned.

72   Another development in Roman Catholic jurisprudence concerns the practice of annulment, that is, the declaration of the fact that a true marriage never existed. The marriage contract requires full and free consent. If this is lacking, there can be no marriage. It has always been recognised that there can be no marriage if a person is forced to enter it against his or her own will. More recent reflection has analysed in greater depth the nature of consent. It is now recognised that there may be serious psychological as well as physical defects. If such defects can be demonstrated to have existed when verbal consent was exchanged, it can be declared, according to Roman Catholic teaching, that there was never a marriage at all (cf CIC Can. 1095). Serious defect is also present if, at the time of exchanging consent, there is a deliberate rejection of some element essential to marriage (cf CIC Can. 1056; 1101, para. 2).

(c)   The Situation Today

73   Clearly there are differences of discipline and pastoral practice between Anglicans and Roman Catholics. Some of the factors in our traditions are the result of responses to contingent historical circumstances: for example, the Roman Catholic Church's requirement of the 'form' for valid marriage. However, other elements have deeper roots. When we explore our differences it is to these, in particular, that we must direct our attention. Before doing so, however, it is important to note that

both Communions make provision for marital separation, without excluding the persons concerned, even after civil divorce, from the eucharist.

74   In accord with the western tradition, Anglicans and Roman Catholics believe that the ministers of the marriage are the man and woman themselves, who bring the marriage into being by making a solemn vow and promise of life-long fidelity to each other. Anglicans and Roman Catholics both regard this vow as solemn and binding. Anglicans and Roman Catholics both believe that marriage points to the love of Christ, who bound himself in an irrevocable covenant to his Church, and that therefore marriage is in principle indissoluble. Roman Catholics go on to affirm that the unbreakable bond between Christ and his Church, signified in the union of two baptised persons, in its turn strengthens the marriage bond between husband and wife and renders it absolutely unbreakable, except by death. Other marriages can, in exceptional circumstances, be dissolved. Anglicans, on the other hand, do not make an absolute distinction between marriages of the baptised and other marriages, regarding all marriages as in some sense sacramental. Some Anglicans hold that all marriages are therefore indissoluble. Others, while holding that all marriages are indeed sacramental and are in principle indissoluble, are not persuaded that the marriage bond, even in the case of marriage of the baptised, can never in fact be dissolved.

75   Roman Catholic teaching that, when a sacramental marriage has been consummated, the covenant is irrevocable, is grounded in its understanding of sacramentality, as already outlined. Further, its firm legal framework is judged to be the best protection for the institution of marriage, and thus best to serve the common good of the community, which itself redounds to the true good of the persons concerned. Thus Roman Catholic teaching and law uphold the indissolubility of the marriage covenant, even when the human relationship of love and trust has ceased to exist and there is no practical possibility of recreating it. The Anglican position, though equally concerned with the sacramentality of marriage and the common good of the community, does not necessarily understand these in the same way. Some Anglicans attend more closely to the actual character of the relationship between husband and wife. Where a relationship of mutual love and trust has clearly ceased to exist, and there is no practical possibility of remaking it, the bond itself, they argue, has also ceased to exist. When the past has been forgiven and healed, a new covenant and bond may in good faith be made.

76   Our reflections have brought to the fore an issue of considerable importance. What is the right balance between regard for the person and regard for the institution? The answer must be found within the context of our theology of communion and our understanding of the common good. For the reasons which have been explained, in the Roman Catholic Church the institution of marriage has enjoyed the favour of the law. Marriages are presumed to be valid unless the contrary case can be clearly established. Since Vatican II renewed emphasis has been placed upon the rights and welfare of the individual person, but tensions still remain. A similar tension is felt by Anglicans, although pastoral concern has sometimes inclined them to give priority to the welfare of the individual person over the claims of the institution. History has shown how difficult it is to achieve the right balance.

77   Our shared reflections have made us see more clearly that Anglicans and Roman Catholics are at one in their commitment to following the teaching of Christ on marriage; at one in their understanding of the nature and meaning of marriage; and at one in their concern to reach out to those who suffer as a result of the breakdown of marriage. We agree that marriage is sacramental, although we do not fully agree on how, and this affects our sacramental discipline. Thus, Roman Catholics recognise a special kind of sacramentality in a marriage between baptised persons, which they do not see in other marriages. Anglicans, on the other hand, recognise a sacramentality in all valid marriages. On the level of law and policy, neither the Roman Catholic nor the Anglican practice regarding divorce is free from real or apparent anomalies and ambiguities. While, therefore, there are differences between us concerning marriage after divorce, to isolate those differences from this context of far-reaching agreement and to make them into an insuperable barrier would be a serious and sorry misrepresentation of the true situation.

4 Contraception

78   Both our traditions agree that procreation is one of the divinely intended 'goods' of the institution of marriage. A deliberate decision, therefore, without justifiable reason, to exclude procreation from a marriage is a rejection of this good and a contradiction of the nature of marriage itself. On this also we agree. We are likewise at one in opposing what has been called a 'contraceptive mentality', that is, a selfish preference for immediate satisfaction over the more demanding good of having and raising a family.

79   Both Roman Catholics and Anglicans agree, too, that God calls married couples to 'responsible parenthood'. This refers to a range of moral concerns, which begins with the decision to accept parenthood and goes on to include the nurture, education, support and guidance of children. Decisions about the size of a family raise many questions for both Anglicans and Roman Catholics. Broader questions concerning the pressure of population, poverty, the social and ecological environment, as well as more directly personal questions concerning the couple's material, physical and psychological resources, may arise. Situations exist in which a couple would be morally justified in avoiding bringing children into being. Indeed, there are some circumstances in which it would be morally irresponsible to do so. On this our two Communions are also agreed. We are not agreed, however, on the methods by which this responsibility may be exercised.

80   The disagreement may be summed up as follows. Anglicans understand the good of procreation to be a norm governing the married relationship as a whole. Roman Catholic teaching, on the other hand, requires that each and every act of intercourse should be 'open to procreation' (cf *Humanae Vitae*, 11). This difference of understanding received official expression in 1930. Before this, both Churches would have counselled abstinence for couples who had a justifiable reason to avoid conception. The Lambeth Conference of Anglican bishops, however, resolved in 1930 that 'where there is a clearly felt moral obligation to limit or avoid parenthood, and where there is a morally sound reason for avoiding complete abstinence ... other methods may be used' (Resolution 15). The encyclical of Pope Pius XI *(Casti Connubii,*1930), which was intended among other things as a response to the Lambeth resolution, renewed the traditional Roman Catholic position. In 1968 the teaching was further developed and clarified in Pope Paul VI's encyclical, *Humanae Vitae.* The Lambeth Conference of 1968 reaffirmed the position that had been taken by the 1958 Lambeth Conference. The Roman Catholic position has been frequently reaffirmed since: for example, in the documents *Familiaris Consortio,* 1981, and *Catechism of the Catholic Church,*1992. This teaching belongs to the ordinary magisterium calling for 'religious assent'.

81   The immediate point at issue in this controversy would seem to concern the moral integrity of the act of marital intercourse. Both our traditions agree that this involves the two basic 'goods' of marriage, loving union and procreation. Moral integrity requires that husband and wife

respect both these goods together. For Anglicans, it is sufficient that this respect should characterise the married relationship as a whole; whereas for Roman Catholics, it must characterise each act of sexual intercourse. Anglicans understand the moral principle to be that procreation should not arbitrarily be excluded from the continuing relationship; whereas Roman Catholics hold that there is an unbreakable connexion, willed by God, between the two 'goods' of marriage and the corresponding meanings of marital intercourse, and that therefore they may not be sundered by any direct and deliberate act (cf *Humanae Vitae*, 12).

82   The Roman Catholic doctrine is not simply an authoritative statement of the nature of the integrity of the marital act. The whole teaching on human love and sexuality, continued and developed in *Humanae Vitae*, must be taken into account when considering the Roman Catholic position on this issue. The definition of integrity is founded upon a number of considerations: a way of understanding human persons; the meaning of marital love; the unique dignity of an act which can engender new life; the relationship between human fruitfulness and divine creativity; the special vocation of the married couple; and the requirements of the virtue of marital chastity. Anglicans accept all of these considerations as relevant to determining the integrity of the marital relationship and act. Thus they share the same spectrum of moral and theological considerations. However, they do not accept the arguments Roman Catholics derive from them, nor the conclusions they draw from them regarding the morality of contraception.

5 Other Issues

83   So far in this section we have argued that our disagreements in the areas of marriage, procreation and contraception, areas in which our two Communions have made official but conflicting pronouncements, are on the level of derived conclusions rather than fundamental values. However, as we observed earlier, there are other important issues in the area of sexuality where no official disagreement has been expressed between our two Communions, but where disagreement is nonetheless perceived to exist. Although Anglicans and Roman Catholics may often achieve a common mind and witness on many issues of peace and social justice, nevertheless, it is said, their teaching is irreconcilable on such matters as abortion and homosexual relations. What is more, there are other difficult and potentially divisive issues in the offing, as scientific and technological

expertise develops the unprecedented power to manipulate the basic material, not only of the environment, but also of human life itself.

84   This is not the time or place to discuss such further issues in detail. However, confining ourselves to the two issues of abortion and homosexual relations, we would argue that, in these instances too, the disagreements between us are not on the level of fundamental moral values, but on their implementation in practical judgements.

85   Anglicans have no agreed teaching concerning the precise moment from which the new human life developing in the womb is to be given the full protection due to a human person. Only some Anglicans insist that in all circumstances, and without exception, such protection must extend back to the time of conception. Roman Catholic teaching, on the other hand, is that the human embryo must be treated as a human person from the moment of conception (cf *Donum Vitae*, 1987, and *Declaration on Procured Abortion* 1974). Difference of teaching on this matter cannot but give rise to difference of judgement on what is morally permissible when a tragic conflict occurs between the rights of the mother and the rights of the fetus. Roman Catholic teaching rejects all direct abortion. Among Anglicans the view is to be found that in certain cases direct abortion is morally justifiable. Anglicans and Roman Catholics, however, are at one in their recognition of the sanctity, and right to life, of all human persons, and they share an abhorrence of the growing practice in many countries of abortion on grounds of mere convenience. This agreement on fundamentals is reflected both in pronouncements of bishops and in official documents issued by both Communions (cf *Catechism of the Catholic Church*, 1992, 2270, and *Lambeth Conference Report*, 1930, 16 and 1978, 10).

86   We cannot enter here more fully into this debate, and we do not wish to underestimate the consequences of our disagreement. We wish, however, to affirm once again that Anglicans and Roman Catholics share the same fundamental teaching concerning the mystery of human life and the sanctity of the human person. They also share the same sense of awe and humility in making practical judgements in this area of profound moral complexity. Their differences arise in the way in which they develop and apply fundamental moral teaching. What we have said earlier about our different formulations of the moral law is here relevant (see para. 52). For Roman Catholics, the rejection of abortion is an example of an absolute prohibition. For Anglicans, however, such an absolute and categorical prohibition would not be typical of their moral reasoning.

That is why it is important to set such differences in context. Only then shall we be able to assess their wider implications.

87   In the matter of homosexual relationships a similar situation obtains. Both our Communions affirm the importance and significance of human friendship and affection among men and women, whether married or single. Both affirm that all persons, including those of homosexual orientation, are made in the divine image and share the full dignity of human creatureliness. Both affirm that a faithful and lifelong marriage between a man and a woman provides the normative context for a fully sexual relationship. Both appeal to Scripture and the natural order as the sources of their teaching on this issue. Both reject, therefore, the claim, sometimes made, that homosexual relationships and married relationships are morally equivalent, and equally capable of expressing the right ordering and use of the sexual drive. Such ordering and use, we believe, are an essential aspect of life in Christ. Here again our different approaches to the formulation of law are relevant (cf para. 52). Roman Catholic teaching holds that homosexual activity is 'intrinsically disordered', and concludes that it is always objectively wrong. This affects the kind of pastoral advice that is given to homosexual persons. Anglicans could agree that such activity is disordered; but there may well be differences among them in the consequent moral and pastoral advice they would think it right to offer to those seeking their counsel and direction.

88   Our two Communions have in the past developed their moral teaching and practical and pastoral disciplines in isolation from each other. The differences that have arisen between them are serious, but careful study and consideration has shown us that they are not fundamental. The urgency of the times and the perplexity of the human condition demand that they now do all they can to come together to provide a common witness and guidance for the well-being of humankind and the good of the whole creation.

F TOWARDS SHARED WITNESS

89 We have already seen how divergence between Anglicans and Roman Catholics on matters of practice and official moral teaching has been
aggravated, if not caused, by the historic breach of communion and the
consequent breakdown in communication. Separation has led to estrangement, and estrangement has fostered misperception, misunder-
standing and suspicion. Only in recent times has this process been reversed
and the first determined steps taken along the way to renewed and full
communion.

90 The theme of communion illumines, we believe, not only the reality
of the Church as a worshipping community, but also the form and fullness of Christian life in the world. Indeed, since the Church is called in
Christ to be a sign and sacrament of a renewed humanity, it also illumines
the nature and destiny of human life as such. As ARCIC has affirmed in
Church as Communion:

> to explore the meaning of communion is not only to speak of the Church
> but also to address the world at the heart of its deepest need, for human beings
> long for true community in freedom, justice and peace and for respect of
> human dignity (para. 3)

In this final section, therefore, we return once again to the theme of
communion and consider the light it sheds both on the moral order and
on the Church's moral response.

1 Communion and the Moral Order

91 Communion, we have argued, is a constitutive characteristic of a fully
human life, signifying 'a relationship based on participation in a shared
reality' (cf *Church as Communion,* para. 12). From this perspective the moral
dimension of human life is itself perceived to be fundamentally relational,
determined both by the nature of the reality in which it participates and
by the form appropriate to such participation.

92 Participation of human beings in the life of God, in whom they live
and move and have their being (cf Acts. 17:28), is grounded in their
creation in God's image (cf *Church as Communion* 6). The fundamental
relationship in which they stand, therefore, is their relationship to God,
Creator and goal of all that is, seen and unseen. Created and sustained in
this relationship, they are drawn towards God's absolute goodness, which

they experience as both gift and call. Moral responsibility is a gift of divine grace; the moral imperative is an expression of divine love. When Jesus bids his disciples before all else to seek the kingdom of God (cf Matt 6.33), he tells them also that they are to reflect in their own lives the 'perfection' which belongs to the divine life (cf Matt. 5.48). This call to 'perfection' echoes the Lord's call to the people of Israel to participate in his holiness (cf Lev. 19.2). As such, it does not ignore human fragility, failure and sin; but it does lay bare the full dimensions of a response that reflects the height and breadth and depth of the divine righteousness and love (cf Rom. 8:1-4).

93   Human beings are not purely spiritual beings; they are fashioned out of the dust (cf Gen. 2.7). Created in the image of God, they are shaped by nature and culture, and participate in both the glory and the shame of the human story. Their responsibility to God issues in a responsibility for God's world, and their transformation into the likeness of God embraces their relationships both to the natural world and to one another. Hence no arbitrary boundaries may be set between the good of the individual, the common good of humanity, and the good of the whole created order. The context of the truly human life is the universal and all-embracing rule of God.

94   The world in which human beings participate is a changing world. Science and technology have given them the power, to a degree unforeseen in earlier centuries, to impress their own designs on the natural environment, by adapting the environment to their own needs, by exploiting it and even by destroying it. However, there are ultimate limits to what is possible. Nature is not infinitely malleable. Moreover, not everything that is humanly possible is humanly desirable, or morally right. In many situations, what is sometimes called progress is, as a consequence of human ignorance and arrogance, degrading and destructive. The moral task is to discern how fundamental and eternal values may be expressed and embodied in a world that is subject to continuing change.

95   The world in which human beings participate is not only a changing world; it is also a broken and imperfect world. It is subject to futility and sin, and stands under the judgement of God. Its human structures are distorted by violence and greed. Inevitably, conflicts of value and clashes of interest arise, and situations occur in which the requirements of the moral order are uncertain. Law is enacted and enforced to preserve order and to protect and serve the common good. Admittedly, it can perpetuate inequalities of wealth and power, but its true end is to ensure justice and

peace. At a deeper level, the moral order looks for its fulfilment to a renewal of personal freedom and dignity within a forgiving, healing and caring community.

2 Communion and the Church

96   Life in Christ is a life of communion, to be manifested for the salvation of the world and for the glorification of God the Father. In the fellowship of the Holy Spirit the Church participates in the Son's loving and obedient response to the Father. But even if, in the resurrection of Christ, the new world has already begun, the end is not yet. So the Church continues to pray and prepare for the day when Christ will deliver the kingdom to the Father (cf 1 Cor. 15:24-28) and God will be all in all. In the course of history Anglicans and Roman Catholics have disagreed on certain specific matters of moral teaching and practice, but they continue to hold to the same vision of human nature and destiny fulfilled in Christ. Furthermore, their deep desire to find an honest and faithful resolution of their disagreements is itself evidence of a continuing communion at a more profound level than that on which disagreement has occurred.

97   The Church as communion reflects the communion of the triune God, Father, Son and Holy Spirit (cf John 17:20-22; John 14:16f; 2 Cor. 13:13), and anticipates the fullness of communion in the kingdom of God. Consequently, communion means that members of the Church share a responsibility for discerning the action of the Spirit in the contemporary world, for shaping a truly human response, and for resolving the ensuing moral perplexities with integrity and fidelity to the Gospel. Within this shared responsibility, those who exercise the office of pastor and teacher have the special task of equipping the Church and its members for life in the world, and for guiding and confirming their free and faithful response to the Gospel. The exercise of this authority will itself bear the marks of communion, in so far as a sustained attentiveness to the experience and reflection of the faithful becomes part of the process of making an informed and authoritative judgement. One such example of this under-standing of the inter-action of communion and authority, we suggest, is the careful and sustained process of listening and public consultation which has preceded the publication of some of the pastoral letters of Bishops' Conferences of the Roman Catholic Church in different parts of the world.

98   Communion also means that, where there has been a failure to meet
the claims of the moral order to which the Church bears witness, there will
be a determined attempt to restore the sinner to the life of grace in the
community, thereby allowing the gospel of forgiveness to be proclaimed
even to the greatest of sinners. Anglicans and Roman Catholics share the
conviction that God's righteousness and God's love and mercy are
inseparable (cf *Salvation and the Church*, 17 and 18), and both Communions
continue to exercise a ministry of healing, forgiveness and reconciliation.

3 Towards Moral Integrity and Full Communion

99   Anglicans and Roman Catholics share a deep desire, not only for full
communion, but also for a resolution of the disagreement that exists
between them on certain specific moral issues. The two are related. On
the one hand, seeking a resolution of our disagreements is part of the
process of growing together towards full communion. On the other hand,
only as closer communion leads to deeper understanding and trust can
we hope for a resolution of our disagreements.

100   In order to make an informed and faithful response to the moral
perplexities facing humanity today, Christians must promote a global and
ecumenical perception of fundamental human relationships and values.
Our common vision of humanity in Christ places before us this responsibility, while at the same time requiring us to develop a greater sensitivity
to the different experiences, insights and approaches that are appropriate
to different cultures and contexts. The separation that still exists between
our two Communions is a serious obstacle to the Church's mission and
a darkening of the moral wisdom it may hope to share with the world.

101   Our work together within this Commission has shown us that the
discernment of the precise nature of the moral agreement and disagreement between Anglicans and Roman Catholics is not always an easy task.
One problem we faced was the fact that we often found ourselves
comparing the variety of moral judgements present and permissible
among Anglicans with the official, authoritative teachings of the Roman
Catholic Church. This feature of our discussions was inevitable, given the
differences between our two Communions in the way they understand
and exercise authority. Working together, however, has convinced us that
the disagreements on moral matters, which at present exist between us,
need not constitute an insuperable barrier to progress towards fuller
communion. Painful and perplexing as they are, they do not reveal a

fundamental divergence in our understanding of the moral implications of the Gospel.

102   Continuing study is needed of the differences between us, real or apparent, especially in our understanding and use of the notion of 'law'. A clearer understanding is required of the relation of the concept of law to the concepts of moral order and the common good, and the relation of all these concepts to the vision of human happiness and fulfilment as 'persons-in-community' that we have been given in and through Jesus Christ. However, Anglicans and Roman Catholics do not talk to each other as moral strangers. They both appeal to a shared tradition, and they recognise the same Scriptures as normative of that tradition. They both respect the role of reason in moral discernment. They both give due place to the classic virtue of prudence. We are convinced, therefore, that further exchange between our two traditions on moral questions will serve both the cause of Christian unity and the good of that larger society of which we are all part.

103   We end our document with a specific practical recommendation. We propose that steps should be taken to establish further instruments of co-operation between our two Communions at all levels of church life (especially national and regional), to engage with the serious moral issues confronting humanity today. In view of our common approach to moral reflection, and in the light of the agreements we have already discovered to exist between us, we believe that bilateral discussions between Anglicans and Roman Catholics would be especially valuable.

104   We make this proposal for the following reasons:

Working together on moral issues would be a practical way of expressing the communion we already enjoy, of moving towards full communion, and of understanding more clearly what it entails; without such collaboration we run the risk of increasing divergence.

Moving towards shared witness would contribute significantly to the mission of the Church and allow the light of the Gospel to shine more fully upon the moral perplexities of human existence in today's world.

Having a shared vision of a humanity created in the image of God, we share a common responsibility to challenge society in places where that image is being marred or defaced.

105   We do not underestimate the difficulties that such collaboration would involve. Nevertheless, we dare not continue along our separated ways. Our working and witnessing together to the world is in itself a form of communion. Such deepening communion will enable us to handle our remaining disagreements in a faithful and more creative way. 'He who calls you is faithful, and he will do it' (1 Thess. 5:24).

MEMBERS OF THE COMMISSION

Anglican Members

The Rt Revd Mark Santer, Bishop of Birmingham, UK *(Co-Chairman)*

The Rt Revd John Baycroft, Bishop of Ottawa, Canada

Dr E. Rozanne Elder, Professor of History, University of West Michigan, USA

The Revd Professor Jaci Maraschin, Professor of Theology in the Ecumenical Institute, San Paulo, Brazil

The Revd Dr John Muddiman, Fellow and Tutor in Theology, Mansfield College, Oxford, UK

The Rt Revd Michael Nazir-Ali, General Secretary, Church Missionary Society, London, UK

The Revd Dr Nicholas Sagovsky, Dean of Clare College, Cambridge, UK

The Revd Dr Charles Sherlock, Senior Lecturer, Ridley College, Melbourne, Australia

SECRETARY

The Revd Canon Stephen Platten, Archbishop of Canterbury's Secretary for Ecumenical Affairs

MORALS CONSULTANTS

The Very Revd Dr Peter Baelz, retired Dean of Durham and formerly Professor of Moral and Pastoral Theology, University of Oxford, UK

The Revd Professor Oliver O'Donovan, Professor of Moral and Pastoral Theology, University of Oxford, UK

OBSERVER

The Revd Dr Donald Anderson, Anglican Consultative Council, London, UK

Roman Catholic Members

The Rt Revd Cormac Murphy-O'Connor, Bishop of Arundel and Brighton, UK *(Co-Chairman)*

Sister Sara Butler, Associate Professor of Systematic Theology, University of St Mary of the Lake, Mundelein, Illinois, USA

The Revd Peter Cross, Professor of Systematic Theology, Catholic Theological College, Clayton, Australia

The Revd Dr Adelbert Denaux, Professor, Faculty of Theology, Catholic University, Leuven, Belgium

The Rt Revd Pierre Duprey, Titular Bishop of Thibare, Secretary, Pontifical Council for Promoting Christian Unity, The Vatican

The Revd Brian V. Johnstone CSSR, Professor, Accademia Alphonsiana, Rome, Italy

The Revd Jean M.R. Tillard OP, Professor, Dominican Faculty of Theology, Ottawa, Canada

The Revd Liam Walsh OP, Professor of Dogmatic Theology, University of Fribourg, Switzerland

SECRETARY

The Very Revd Mgr Kevin McDonald, Staff Member, Pontifical Council for Christian Unity, The Vatican (until July 1993)

The Revd Timothy Galligan, Staff Member, Pontifical Council for Christian Unity, The Vatican (from August 1993)

MORALS CONSULTANTS

The Revd Professor Enda McDonagh, Professor of Moral Theology, St Patrick's College, Maynooth, Ireland

The Revd Bruce Williams, OP, Professor of Moral Theology, Pontifical University of St Thomas Aquinas, Rome, Italy

World Council of Churches Observer

The Revd Dr Gunther Gassmann, Director, Faith and Order Commission, WCC, Geneva, Switzerland

'Life in Christ' – Study Pack

A recent study carried out by the English Anglican – Roman Catholic Committee (ARC) revealed a wide understanding of the issues considered by ARCIC even though the reports have not been widely read at parish level.

English ARC have produced a study pack to accompany this ARCIC report. It contains a short tape with comments by the ARCIC Co-Chairmen and material drawn from the *Life in Christ* report, suitable for parish or ecumenical discussion groups.

Available from Church House Bookshop, 31 Great Smith Street, London SW1P 3BN or all good religious bookshops.